The Jack of Diamonds Is a Hard Card to Play

The Jack of Diamonds Is a Hard Card to Play

Paul Christensen

Copyright © 2015 Paul Christensen
All Rights Reserved

ISBN: 978-1-942956-11-2
Library of Congress Control Number: 2015949781

Mixed media cover art by Maxine Christensen
Cover design by Elie Monge.
Manufactured in the United States

Lamar University Literary Press
Beaumont, Texas

In Memory of

R. G. Vliet

poet and novelist
1929-1984

Poetry from Lamar University Literary Press

Alan Berecka, *With Our Baggage*
David Bowles, *Flower, Song, Dance: Aztec and Mayan Poetry*
Jerry Bradley, *Crownfeathers and Effigies*
Chip Dameron, *Waiting for an Etcher*
William Virgil Davis, *The Bones Poems*
Jeffrey DeLotto, *Voices Writ in Sand*
Mimi Ferebee, *Wildfires and Atmospheric Memories*
Larry Griffin, *Cedar Plums*
Ken Hada, *Margaritas and Redfish*
Michelle Hartman, *Disenchanted and Disgruntled*
Michelle Hartman, *Irony and Irreverence*
Katherine Hoerth, *Goddess Wears Cowboy Boots*
Lynn Hoggard, *Motherland*
Gretchen Johnson, *A Trip Through Downer, Minnesota*
Ulf Kirchdorfer, *Chewing Green Leaves*
Janet McCann, *The Crone at the Casino*
Erin Murphy, *Ancilla*
Laurence Musgrove, *Local Bird*
Dave Oliphant, *The Pilgrimage, Selected Poems: 1962-2012*
Kornelijus Platelis, *Solitary Architectures*
Carol Coffee Reposa, *Underground Musicians*
Jan Seale, *The Parkinson Poems*
Carol Smallwood, *Water, Earth, Air, Fire, and Picket Fences*
Glen Sorestad *Hazards of Eden*
W.K. Stratton, *Ranchero Ford/ Dying in Red Dirt Country*
Wally Swist, *Invocation*
Jonas Zdanys (ed.), *Pushing the Envelope, Epistolary Poems*

For information on these and other Lamar University Literary press books go to
www.Lamar.edu/literarypress

A cattle trail drunk and a hard road to travel
That old Jack O' Diamonds is a hard card to play
Get along, get along, get along little doggies
Get along little doggies and be on your way

Woodie Guthrie's version

CONTENTS

I

13 Jack of Diamonds
18 Rain Storm
20 Between Smyrna and Babylon
22 North of Waco
24 Thoughts Before My Nap
26 Two Strangers at a Corner
27 My Advice to You
29 Inventory of the Birds in My Yard
31 An Ordinary Morning in Austin
33 In a Pasture on the Way to Victoria
35 Passing through Hearne
37 Around Ten at Night
39 Another Sleepless Night
41 The Parable of the Pig

II

45 The Hero of the West
47 The Bryan Reading Club
48 Walmart
50 Divided Loyalties
52 Journey toward Dawn
54 On I-10, Driving to New Orleans
56 Scorpion Cave
57 The Place of Judgment
58 At the Dallas Car Lot
61 A Friend of Mine
62 Girls Taking Showers at the Summer Camp
63 After Sunday Service
65 The Ugly Land
67 What the Poor Are Doing in Texas
68 At Home

III

73   I Used to Be So Sure About You
75   Old Friends and Poets
77   A Dinner Party in the Hills
79   Moses on the Outskirts of Austin
81   Let's Build some Temples
82   Thirteen Ways of Looking at a Grackle
84   The Geography of the Brain
85   At Night I Give Up My Soul
86   The Man Who Talked Too Much
87   Chores
89   Walking behind Terlingua
90   Love and Death
91   To Grow Old in Texas
93   The Hunt
95   A West Texas Marriage
97   Is It Ten O'Clock Yet?
98   The Cascades of Autumn
100 A Poem for My Father
102 In the Depths behind El Paso
104 The Loneliest Tuesday of the Year

I

Jack of Diamonds

They say the diamond suit in a deck
of playing cards comes from spears;
a knave was chosen from among lancers
to be a vassal, and serve his lord in war.
So he was Jack o' Spears, or Shakespeare?
False lead. The spears became guns
in the old hardpan towns of Texas,
when the bar room was the only church in town.
Among the murmurs of that
holy congregation of gamblers
and taxi girls, bloodless Jack sat
brooding over his hand, two pair
and a jack high, across from the master
of stone face, the magician with more aces
up his sleeve than Satan. He threw
in his Stetson, spurs, his saddle,
and a wad of soiled pesos
to make his bet. The old man's wattles
shook like a turkey's, his only sign
he might be worried. He had
his rights to a brown river on the table.
He was all for pushing his wife
into the mix, but she was home
nursing a newborn, whose was a question.

"I call," said Jack, and tilted his chair
against the wall. The eaves were dark
with crows and buzzards, and down
at the livery stable you could hear
two men ripping planks with a hand saw.
The breeze lifted the dust off
the hills behind, and the blue sky

was lighter by a hue, like a widow's veil
hung over the noon sun. The town
held its breath, and nothing rose
from the silence but the sound
of a man sinking nails into a coffin.
The barkeep brought shots of rye
and said they were on the house.
Maybe he had spades, or four
hearts and Ace high for a flush.
No telling what the old sharp
could pull from his soiled fingers
and fling down, and use his hat
to plow the winnings up.
But he had more crows' feet in his eyes
than were crows on the ridge poles.
He looked tired; like he had used up
all his bullets and let the coyotes eat
the rest of the steer carcass. He was bone
dry, his chest rattling like a squeeze box
as he considered how to shoot poor Jack,
who didn't have a gun. Maybe someone
handed him one when he wasn't looking,
but this is Argus of the hundred eyes
who misses nothing at a game table.

Louise sat there in her fiery red dress,
legs crossed on the bar, net stockings
with a run down one calf, and high heels
looking like they could use a shod.
She nursed a cup of corn liquor
swirling with road dust. The floor
creaked under the wind buffets,
and the sign over the notary's office
wheezed like an asthmatic.

Everything needed oil; nothing worked
the way it used to. Even the fiddle
was broken and hung from a hook
over the piano. The hill outside rose
out of the dry land like a banker's
darkest thoughts, as he locked up
and headed home. Could be things
would improve in time, could be.
He didn't think so, and kept his silence.
But the guns behind him might
carve a hole in the muted hour
and the drunks run rampage.
You had to think things through,
he said, sitting down to lunch.

Jack was as lean as a briar switch
and mean as mesquite thorns;
he ate rattlesnake when no one else
could stomach what he called chicken meat,
and saw the Union soldiers swarm
over the ridge and descend in a blur
white as a cotton field shooting
their muskets off. Everyone was dying
as he pushed his greasy meal
into the fire, and rolled down
into the shade of a dry gulley.
He was took for dead, he said later.

Then he rode west without his grays,
just a torn shirt he found in a graveyard.
Pants he made from a saddle blanket
someone left behind. He was the new South,
blood bitter, mind empty as
a creek's bed in the pitch of summer.

He was eager to try his luck at Indian fighting
but the wars were almost over.
The flag of the Confederacy hung in tatters
from a pole, with a burned house beside it.
Time moves slowly in the desert,
as if carried on a turtle's back.

But Jack put down his cards and the breath
whistled through a lot of whiskers;
no one could believe he had a winning hand.
The old man smiled for the first time,
as if he had five aces to unfold.
But what he put down was a pair
of fours, a king, and two orphans
from another suit. The girls came down
the steps halfway, waiting for the shots
to ring against the tin-plate ceiling.
But there was only silence,
eerie as a snake's thoughts. And then
the men shook hands, and the master
walked away. Wind played a broken flute
all evening, and the boys went home sober.
For the first time anyone could remember
a man with a wild jack took the table.

On the hill where Jack's bones are buried,
someone carved a diamond on a wooden cross,
and even the toddlers knew what it signified
as they passed on the way to church.
In this cracked land, fissured like
an old man's worried face, lingered
the ashes of hope, and a rattle
like dice in the dry weeds. The saloon
closed, the rails came through,

the stark, burnt, hollow core of some
abandoned paradise lingered
in the glare, a squandered dream.
Rye whiskey in your throat, a road
leading nowhere, a camp fire long gone out.

In the end, the desert eats your dreams,
stone huts, broken temples, and all.
The sound that remains is of a woman
singing all alone, on the side of a hill,
strumming her lyre and lamenting
the vanity of all things.

Rain Storm

Rolls of thunder sound like an old man
coughing up his life. Big troughs
of silence intervene, sucking the air
out of the stifling daylight.
The field shivers in a sudden fever
as the wind ripples drunkenly
out of nowhere, a bad uncle come
home after a long bitter feud
with the family. He's here now,
sprawled on the sofa, drying out
with moans and spasms, his dirty
blue suit rising up his legs as he turns
and shouts into the dusty pillows.
A storm sweeps him up into the rest
of the hallucinations gathering in the sky.

There was no warning, people say,
peering out of the plate glass window
of the hardware store. The cars are melting
into watery illusions in the parking lot.
The dusty ruler-edge of reality slithers
down the muddy gutters. Trees hold up
their leaves like blind beggars, tangled
in pain from the long dry months.
A man is running across an intersection
with a newspaper flapping and soggy
on his head. He is as lost as we are.
Suddenly, we are in an empty universe
but for the chaos overhead, the loose granite
falling in slabs from imaginary mountains.
Heaven dismantling its castle in a shock
of earthquake jerks, as the sky convulses,

vomits a torrent of gray language no one
can make sense of. Deaf and dumb,
we cringe like children in a war.

Between Smyrna and Babylon

Can the Post Oak Mall quench
my soul's thirst? I am a man in a linoleum
and drywall desert, wandering
in the footsteps of the old fathers,
long vanished from the offset-
shadowless maze. I have found
the ancient alphabet lodged
in a cranny of a wall, between
the nail salon and Radio Shack.
I ponder it long and long.

I am a wanderer in the bitter
light, a blinded pilgrim inching
my way forward on the sound
of whispers and gossip, loud bursts
of laughter, caustic denunciations
of one another. Love perished
on these shores, and in these
embittered arroyos; the sunglass
peddler's stall drifts like
Noah's ark in the middle
of a sea of anxiety and regrets.

All my life I cradled my heart
in calloused hands. I tender
it to you, total stranger,
who may or may not need my love.
But what can we buy that we
don't already own? And what
is there worth dying for
that lies shrink-wrapped on the shelf?
Tell me if redemption

is possible with a coupon?
Have you seen the shoes on sale?
Could they take us to the Promised Land?

North of Waco

No one remembers a thing these days.
One day is stitched into memory
like any other, selvage-frayed, indistinguishable
as ranch-type houses on a hill.
I'd hate to be a drunk coming
home from the sales conference
with my key in hand, looking
for a door lost among the corn rows
of brick and hedges, driveways
and lawn sprinklers, bikes
upended near the garage door.
One of them is mine, I whisper
in a slur, if only I knew the secret
combination of my life, and where
I hid my family before I left.

The hum of existence is
like a bluebottle's flight. It arises
from the motors that impel
us to go on living. The secret
heart of a refrigerator prays
to the god of electric things,
and the vent overhead pours
out the lamentations of Ruth
and Naomi, the weeping voice
of La Llorona, calling for her
children in the crackling weeds.

Freedom begins in the stuttering
of the clock, the silence between
each jerk of the minute hand.
I know that. I can't talk about it.

It's something my wife lets me
conceal from her. The hidden
dimension I retreat to
at night when she sleeps, and I
am left awake to ponder
the burning stars, the tug of
the moon to free itself from earth.
When the moon is gone, in that
hesitation of eternity's gold watch,
I know the earth will go on
like a ghost in the dark,
asking questions no one can answer.

Thoughts before My Nap

Years ago, when I could draw in my belt
to the last notch, and lean down to tie
my shoes without gasping, life
was sweeter, as plump
as a waitress in the Fox & Hound.

I grow old, and my heart is tired
of reminding me to breathe.
I gaze upon the ruin that was my house
of mirth, and the mirror winces.
It offers me a drink, but if I take it,
I won't sleep tonight. I must
grow strong in will, even if my spirit
has gone to bed, and lies
there like a neglected wife.

I used to wear a hat; I never forgot
to take along an umbrella, even
though it had not rained in years.
When the earth shriveled and cracked,
and the lawn died, the heat stood
like all the ghosts of the Civil War
in the attic. Then all things came
loose from their place,
but I stood firm. I had a purpose.

I was young, full of noise
I translated into ambition. So did
everyone else. We were the bold ones,
the strikers, the thugs of Wall Street,
the apes descending
upon civilization from the wild fig trees,

the criers in the night jungle, the hairy
chested bullies, the muscular
bosses, the ones ordering the earth
to do our bidding.
God I miss those days. All we are
are fools, sad, wrinkled fools
peering through the slats of the blinds
at a world we couldn't change.

Two Strangers at the Corner

Ask a man the weather, and he will
look at the sky, as if change could
only come from clouds
and wind. He doesn't think
much; he's a stranger in the world
even though he can count three friends
he'd share his dinner with.

Ask a man the time, and he consults
his watch, not the liver spots
on his wrist, or the weak pulse
stumbling in his arm.
He hasn't a clue where death
lurks, or when it might come
down from its hiding place.

Ask a man for directions, and he
unfolds his map. But all I wanted
to know was how to save my life.
He thinks I'm lost, but I don't
interrupt his thoughts to tell him
how far at sea I find myself.
I love this man; he had read
the surface of his life and found
it full of numbers and arrows.

He was not meant to question
the dark enclosing us,
the cold breath of the graveyard
raising the hackles on our necks.
He thinks he might belong,
that he deserves to sleep in his bed tonight.
I wish him well and move along.

My Advice to You

A path is a dent in the earth
where feet have formed their habits.
Nothing more. Don't follow it
even if you're late to something.

Try the unmowed grass
of the field behind you,
the slight upheave of earth
forming a breast under the sky.
Try the hip at the top, the slender
leg that extends itself
down to the small, running creek
where nature whispers to itself.

Or try the wind, with its
fragrant breath, the song it sings
as you become liberated
from your obligations.

    * * *

You're nothing in this world,
good friend. Not even the smallest
pebble owes you a favor.
The trees don't even know
when you pass beneath them.

You're just you, a molecule
with a name and an overcoat.
You're a forked bone, a stomach
always growling for a meal,
a mouth flapping out distortions

of the world, a pair of eyes
that see the same old thing each morning.

  * * *

You see that light at the bottom
of the street? It paints the dark
a grayish color, and smoothes
away the contradictions long enough
for you to make it home.
That's your biography, chum,
written in the dent of your sofa,
the worn place in your dinner table
where you park your elbows.
When your daughter asks you
if there is a god, don't answer.
You don't know. You never asked.

Inventory of the Birds in My Yard

A robin that memorized twelve
caroling trills and thirty whisper notes
observes a mockingbird in the next tree.
The mockingbird sets up his music stand,
polishes his beak, clears a seed from
his throat, and begins to warble
like Weird Al Yankovic on acid.
The robin blinks, shuffles his big feet,
and makes a long face.
It's some two-bit sonata written
by a schoolboy, a recitation
of the Gettysburg Address by a man
pacing in a circle at the state asylum.

The mockingbird hears nothing
but the sweetness of his own voice.
He sings and sings and the earth goes
on merrily orbiting. The blue jay
makes an illiterate screech now and then
to mark the passing of the sun.
The grackle breaks a pane of glass
every time he clears his throat.
The turkey buzzard belches up carrion between
the notes of his pathetic dirge.

The robin is unmoved. He has a repertoire
that never changes. Oh, maybe a
variation here and there depending
on the weather, or if he's had sex
with a stranger recently. He might
let a little eros into his heart, and
belt out a serenade if he's

on the streets again. The robin
is my hero, my vaudeville tramp
in spats and top hat, my buddy
all summer long—a regular guy
who will stand you to a drink
and act like it's nothing when he
nails an Irish ballad at the piano.

An Ordinary Morning in Austin

You see them slaving away
in a boiler room, men and women
banging on keyboards, staring
into the death's head of a monitor
looking for a trend. You feel
queasy peering in from the street,
shielding the sun from your eyes.
You're hungry, maybe want a drink.
But it's only ten o'clock, and Austin
throbs with energy it can't burn.

So you stand there like some
uncle in an old sepia photograph,
your trousers luffing in the wind,
revealing your skinny legs
and old-fashioned two-tone shoes.
You wish you were just waking
up in Shanghai a hundred years ago,
smelling the won ton soup from
the stall below. You wish you were
a girl playing hopscotch on a London street.
You wish a lot of things you can't have
and go on staring, chewing an imaginary
blade of grass as you gaze.

How can someone so young,
so ready to embrace her life
lean forward with her coffee cup
and doubt her calculations,
blowing a strand of golden hair
from her brow as she pouts a moment?
She won't ask her colleagues for a clue

because they're all competing for a raise.
She's like some beautiful bolt
screwed down under the cowling of a
motor, turning slowly with the wheel
she's on, elegant as a nickel-plated
lug doing a job no one notices.

Or him in the corner, the dreamer,
drifting around in a half-formed
fantasy about a river, a fly rod
in his hand, the sound of thunder
far off, the smell of ozone after
the first streak of lightning
cracks the sky wide open to outer space.
He can't help it; it's summer, and his blood
cries out for fish, and a camp fire,
a drum pounding in the darkness
he can't quite distinguish from
a bull frog chanting his desire.

In a Pasture on the Way to Victoria

I admire Plato up there on his hill
chewing grass, thinking about
the forms of nature that lie
just beyond his mental reach.
He has a brahma hump he scratches
on a post, and his nose,
wet as a glossy creek's skin,
detects a sleek white cow nearby.

He has to think through something
Socrates once said, about a youth
who dared not look too deeply
into his soul, lest he find the minotaur.
There's a meaning there, a kind of message
at the bottom of a canyon,
something to remind you that all
that rises and illuminates an afternoon
is not real, only a guise of nature
worn like a veil over the face
of a beautiful Arab girl.

Plato lies there in the shadow
of a gnarled yaupon, among
Indian blanket, high Johnson
grass that awaits his meditative jaw.
He has reasoned with the best of them.
His eyes contain worlds beyond
whatever Hamlet dreamt; he has been
to the Jordan with the saints,
and walked among the prophets.

He was once a man like you and me,
and he married the daughter of King Solomon.
He lived in the silk and oil-lantern
glitter of a desert palace, and beheld night
acrawl with visions. He listened
to the muses and begged them
to take him up to meet the gods,
but they were giggling like schoolgirls.
When he dared to question what they knew,
someone threw a thunderbolt
and he sprouted horns, and hooves,
his four-chambered paunch,
and there he sat, in the palm of a thousand
years of ignorance, the dust
of Atlantis on his tongue, and the
secret path to heaven long forgotten.

Passing through Hearne

The old cotton towns crumble
under the weight of guilt;
a skeletal cart is parked
in the shadow of the past.
But the voices can't be stilled.
They come awake each
evening when the wind rises.
You hear their chants in the field.
You sense the crack of the whip
each time a freight train hits
a gap in the rails.
You know a white man
is eating his anger even now,
in a kitchen at twilight,
his wife at the stove stirring
hope in a blackened pan.

Memory has legs and moves
in the cracks of time;
its odor lingers in the living room,
in the dusty settle that has not moved
in a century of troubled nights.
A silver fork lies tarnished
in a drawer, the color of steel
that lost its bright reflection.
A piano can't strike its own keys;
the hands that played are dust.
The bones of the master class
are buried on the hill, under
the forgiving yew trees.

Doesn't matter. Nothing can erase
the blood stains, the sweat,
the terror of ownership, the
justice that banged its gavel
on a block of oak, and demanded death.
The old towns creak, and loose
boards chatter of the past,
and the diner where farmers
lean down into their morning eggs
is haunted by an oak where
bodies hung with blood-shot eyes.

Around Ten at Night

A mosquito's only purpose
is to remind us that god is not perfect.

It borrows a pinhead's worth of blood
and leaves a welt for receipt.

I scratch at it on my porch,
a cold gin and tonic perched on my knee.

I was beginning to drift
with the night, when the sting occurred.

I had forgotten about malice, about
the debits and errors of this life.

I had become sedate and naïve
once more in the bubble I wear around me.

I had thought of this earth as home;
it rocked me in its mothering arms.

I was deserving of its kindness,
having led my life narrowly.

An angel flew over me
and left behind a path of stars.

My heart found its voice
and began to sing. I had not heard

this song since childhood,
the rhymes of Eden on my tongue.

And then a bullet shot from god's own rifle
sunk its fang into my arm and left me

shaking, the house of faith I built
from straw was set ablaze with bitter questions.

Another Sleepless Night

Angels tramp across my eyelids
on their way to the front.
The war is breaking out again,
in the corners of bedrooms,
in the stillness of the pots
in the kitchen. In the garage,
where the rags stink of despair.

Now I am awake once more.
Lying there like a board
breathing through its knots.
I feel my dry sap glisten
in the moonlight. I am intrigued
by my memories of being a tree
in the forest, with birds in my hair.
Before the war, I mean.
Before the axes fell against us.

There is no wilderness wider
than a postage stamp; the worms
have inherited the earth.
We have devoured the future
in a banquet of greed and lust.
Now only the smoke remains
of our thirst for wealth.
Birds sing the history we have erased.

In a field near here, below my
bedroom window, stumps
mark the progress of civilization.
A red brick marks the gate to an old
kingdom of ideas; a slab

of disintegrating iron
sums up the Industrial Revolution.
My diary is composed of
ghosts trying to find their homes.

The Parable of the Pig

Two cousins tamed a wild pig
and taught her how to dance.
She rose up on hind legs, pink
belly as fair as any maiden's cheek,
and on the tips of her
delicate, pixelated legs

she reenacted the Italian Renaissance.
It was a thrill to watch.
You would have paid a price
to see such elegance
in this fallen world.
Behind her rose the oilrigs
into the night's choked air.

They took her to the market towns
to show the reach
of her exquisite consciousness.
She wore a bonnet of Peruvian
straw with a rose pinned to the brim,
and flashed her sultry eyes
at all the hunger sitting there.
She had transcended bacon
to climb high culture's golden stair.

All our flights of imagination
were mimicked in her whirling
steps, her pirouettes on a balcony,
her leaps into the angel-haunted
air to carry her to the limit
of human longing. She would
hover there, over the heads

of her admiring audience,
the perfect metaphor of the need
to fool ourselves and all of nature.

II

The Hero of the West

Every man is a landmine
waiting to explode.
He keeps his secrets
to himself, buried
in his chest, where the heart
languishes in silence.
He will not divulge a single
secret he has nourished
with his spit. He knows
things even he can't know.

Secrets abound in him,
under his sweat-stained
Stetson, under his soiled
collar, itching him under
his tooled belt and clay-
caked jeans. His boots
carry the weight of
stifled emotions on heels,
an inch or two above
the earth. He is the very
model of a thing disconnected
from the world, solid,
defiant, gun-protected,
eager to die before a word
escaped from the dungeon
in his throat. He smiles
and turns his burnt eyes
to the sun; he has a side-
hitched gait from living
on a horse. He can't tell
the difference between a stone

and a woman's lips, unless
he thinks he can seduce her.

It's all about the masculinity,
you know. The rawhide
binding the heart to his ribs
to keep it from fleeing
makes him friend
to other lonely men.
He has no home to rest
his soul within, only
a bed where the springs
sing to him of loneliness.

The Bryan Reading Club

They're not widows anymore, once
the pocket doors are shut, and copies
of *Women in Love* come out to
rest upon their skinny knees.

Long bony fingers prod the lush
English sentences where a woman
fell into an embrace and let
her lover in, and rolled herself to ecstasy.

The parlor clock ticks; the traffic
outside is as dry as cricket song;
the freight train threatens to wreck
the sky with its diesel horn
as it grinds silence under the wheels.

But the talk is soft, insistent,
the analysis bright as a glass of water.
One old crone leans forward
as if to adjust her glasses
before admitting that the joys
of love are as fresh now
as when she was a bride.

Ah yes. All that was once the
fire of girlhood waits in their
imaginations, and words
hold up a match to the dry straw.
The body's beauty outshines the sun.
There is no darkness that can
extinguish the flames engulfing them.

Walmart

At night, sometimes late at night,
Walmart becomes democracy,
the one America craves in its
revolutionary dreams, its fervid
documents. The doors burst with
light, and the aisles are thronged
with freaks, doddering couples
hanging on to their shopping cart
to keep from falling. I saw a woman
held up by her two skinny daughters,
the fattest woman in the world.
But her daughters loved her,
and they guided her down the rows
of fruit juice as if she were
the Statue of Liberty
out on the town for the night.

A young couple caked in grease
and dirt from a long day at the garage
moved stealthily, keeping out of
range of everyone's stares,
but even in their filthy clothes
they read the labels carefully,
wishing to avoid the bad chemicals.
A tall man, Uncle Sam himself
in blue jeans and a sleeveless shirt,
moved down the aisles
as if they were golden rows
of Kansas corn, or the sweet
lofty grasses of the Great Plains
before the white man came.
He was proud, with hard eyes

and a head as noble as Lincoln's.
He too hungered for the manna
of America.

They were all here; the kids,
the shop lifters, thugs in jackets,
a gang member with a missing tooth,
the prostitute tired of standing
in the movie parking lot.
The dreamers, the liars, cutthroats
with a knife bulging in a front pocket.
The newly divorced woman with
hungry eyes; the basketball
player who warmed the bench all season,
the high school teacher, the fat pawn
broker with a pocketful of worn out money.
They too found their names inscribed
on the great tablets of freedom, and walked
with straight backs into the glare
and chaos of so much plenty.

The tills rang like the 4th of July;
floor walkers kept their snake's eyes
beaded, as the girl with braces
is hauled off to the holding room
with her stolen lipstick in a matron's fist.
God bless you all, I say, as I stroll
with empty cart, just happy to be here.

Divided Loyalties

Laredo sprawls over the muddy Rio Grande
like a serape, the edge of one dream dangling
its wool into the beginning of another.

Over the treetops, a second world shimmers
in the heat. The earth is browner,
trees mangier, like the coast of Africa

or the plains of Panama. It's hot
under the branches of Laredo's
palms, the painted trunks of locusts.

Here we are running out of vocabulary,
my English growing thicker as I try to speak,
my teeth biting into the pulp of a verb.

I smell onions, the salsa bubbling
in a pan, an exhaust fan rattling
with greasy air, the tang of frying cactus leaves.

We meet and divide here. The Kickapoos
were forced to take shelter on an island
in the dwindling water of the river,

and Zach Taylor held them there.
Irish regulars stared back
at the north country, their rifles

raised, their tawny native wives
eager to charge the banks,
to defend Mexico's wounded borders.

But fate, as William Carlos Williams said,
played out its hand, one ace
after the other, in a game of stud.

There was no way to win this war,
and the dreams separated like
two Siamese heads split down the middle

of a river bed, a fractured spine,
the disconnected nerves, two religions,
two races, two brothers blown apart.

But my heart longs for both of them.
I am as much the child of dry
fields and prickly pear as I am

the native son of the north.
I cannot let one go for the other.
The night is soft and musical, I hear

the guitars from over here, standing
with the night caressing me,
with the fajita smoke hanging in the air,
the laughter that only comes from tragedy.

Journey toward Dawn

Trees eat the light overhead
as I walk deeper into the woods.
I follow the meanderings of a creek,
whose switch-back progress
reminds me of the wanderings
of a turtle. Boulders keep the water
from escaping too far. The paws
of dogs and rabbits dapple
the soft brown banks.

This is the hand of some benign
spirit pouring its blood
into the thirsty land.
We cannot help but follow
where it goes, as if it led
to heaven's door.

A couple is making love
in a tent; their voices
are like echoes of each other,
as they gulp air and struggle
to reach that jittery nirvana of love.
I wish them well.
Ahead, more adventures
in the shape of rocks
dotted with reptile prints.
We're going backward into time,
like walking in a telescope
toward the sky. The past keeps
intervening in my thoughts
showing me its treasures
from a time in which my dust
had not yet mingled with my ancestors.

The text I read, page by rocky
page, is full of scree and lizard
tracks, the gloomy smell
of time standing still
in its empty cave. The birds
hang in the sky, the wild game
hidden everywhere, with eyes
like pebbles if one could only
peer deep enough into the shadows.

On I-10, Driving to New Orleans

I'm told they still sell toy gallows
at the fair in Blue, Texas, near the border
with Louisiana. Not far away
is the more notorious Vidor,
capital of racist East Texas,
"sundown town," for the curfew
imposed on blacks during Jim Crow,
and where the Ku Klux Klan
met (and still does) to burn crosses.

It was logged out by a lumber
baron, King Vidor (not the director),
and settled back into the marshes
of history. Not like Jasper,
where James Byrd, Jr. was dragged
behind a pickup truck for miles
until mere bone and skin,
and dead. That put Jasper on the map.
Tough towns, with only
a fraction of blacks daring to live
among the vast majority of whites.
You drive with your heart in
your mouth, afraid of a flat tire
or a broken tie rod. You don't want
to stay, even if you're white.

You smell the cauldron of racial
hate as you speed along,
the coastal air full of salt
and bitterness, the sense
you have reached the end
of the world, the beginning of

hell—a plain of stilted houses,
rice farms, fishing shacks, broken
marriages, the soiled heavens
blown west by refineries
and chemical plants. You don't
want to eat here, or stay overnight.

You pray for the first time
in years that you will not be
stopped by cops or a truck load
of rednecks shouting *nigger lover!*
But you move along, careful
to stay between the yellow lines,
a clean and Christian soul
worthy of the love of other pious men.

We shall all rejoice in bringing in the sheaves.

Scorpion Cave

We were standing above a painted cave
on the Pecos River, the so-called
"Panther Cave" from the figure
painted in vegetable dyes on the wall
of the cave, smudged by ancient fires
to mark the seasons of the year
and the start of the bison hunt.

Some diggeroes, hired help who
do all the digging for the archaeologists,
had made a fire and were eating
supper, passing a wine bottle
back and forth. We smoked
and chatted, and I was ready to go to bed
when I looked up. A starry sky
hung over us, close enough
to touch. "What's that," I said,
pointing at a gathering of stars,
"That's Scorpio," a man said,
handing back the wine bottle.
"Scorpio? Wow, I almost thought
it was a panther by its shape."

"If the painters were copying
the sky from the river, couldn't
that just be Scorpio reversed?"
No one answered me. But somewhere,
some time there will be an article
published on re-naming this
beautiful limestone hunters' cave.

The Place of Judgment

Some friendly soul wandered too far
and ended up a cactus, out on the west
side of the hill, among the broken stone
and the vomit of time's memories.
It lingers there, flat-eared and needled,
its moisture hoarded in a lung
buried deep behind its heart.

Some god took vengeance on a mortal's pride
and shot his thunderbolt, caught
the poor man's breath before it left his soul.
He erred against the laws, or let his
mind wander into forbidden gardens,
a moist place on which to nourish
one's perishable mortality a little while.

What's in your pocket at this moment,
I ask? Some coins, a folded bill
for getting you to tomorrow?
Here's the moral landscape folded
like a treasure map, creased
here and there with scars
of old abandoned rivers. The heaves
of ground are there to try your character,
your willingness to suffer and be good.

At the Dallas Car Lot

You want to buy the car. It shines
like a meteor in the sky.
It has powerful sides, like a
gladiator's. It will die if no one
sends it careering down a freeway soon.
It was not meant to collect the shadows
of the lot. The seats are
leather and can strap you in
as you gain momentum
and dodge the planets in your way.
Your soul was born for an odyssey,
a trek to the distant edge
of vision. You know this is your baby,
it calls your name with a coy rattle
of its starter motor, a growl
of lust and desire as the engine idles.

There it stands, with a bank nearby
ready to lend you the money for adventure.
The salesman is young, still in his acne
years, his collar loose around his long neck.
He has seduced a dozen starving hearts
this week, and here's another,
eager to hear some sweet talk,
to have his problems pushed to the back
of his head, and a vision to nourish in his eyes.
The salesman is a poet; he has honey breath,
like Pindar. When he sleeps in the yard,
the bees hover at his mouth.
He has seen stout souls with Scottish pocketbooks
fall into a drunken stupor at his words,
and kneel in the noon sun begging

for the keys. The keys are jingling,
the keys are like every dazzling idea
that has won an argument.

Still you hesitate. And then he says,
"Americans can't live without a road
under them, tires eating up the past,
some horizon that sings like a siren
to you. You're just an ordinary man
on foot until you slide behind the wheel.
Then the nation stands up to you,
makes the mountains part, the women
cry out from their bedrooms to marry them.
You're just a landlubber until you feel
the gale on your face, your sleeves
puffing up like the sails of Odysseus' ship.
You're a hero going over the line,
heading into unknown seas.
You're the man who can save this world,
soiled and beaten as it is.
You alone in a chrome chariot
with a spear and shield, a checkbook
in your back pocket, a heart as full
as Midas' purse. So buy it, rejoice,
and let us conquer space!"

Yes, you say, yes. I'll sign the papers.
This is all mine, you cry, leaning against
the bright metallic blue fender,
looking into the coffee-colored enchantments
of the front seat, with its knobs
and toggles, its gauges, the grinning
face of a radio, the controls of the air conditioner.
Oh God, yes! Speed, freedom, liberation

from the burdens of my life. My heart
is unpacking its suitcase of old sorrows
as I speak. Nothing on land can hold me now.
I am ready, Moses, to lead the Jews.

When you are home, sitting in the driveway
with your purchase, your suspicious eye
traces the blister of a plastic rim
on the steering wheel, and the smooth
bald edge of the brake pedal. You note
the smudge on the inside of the odometer
when someone was in there fixing something.
You are like an old man sitting on the side
of the bed in some brothel in Istanbul,
ruing the night before, lamenting his empty
purse, the poor woman pulling up her stockings
and giving you a look of disapproval.

A Friend of Mine

I know a man who confides his sorrows
in his horse. The large black eyes
stare back at him, and if there were
arms to wrap him in her compassion
she would have taken him to bed.

Instead, he shoulders his grief
and moves alone into the future,
a gauntly-dimensioned
pilgrim of the land. He masters
little in his domain, with a stunted
reach into the mysteries of nature.

He knows there are powers
that dwarf his meager height
and alter his fate each time he wakes.
He has no hope that he can
master life, and turns instead
to his black mare, with her flashing
mane and lofty concentration.

Perhaps she can help. She's so much
closer to the doors of night, and
the soft, pliant give of nurturing earth.
She is his soul at times, and he
a mind exiled in thought,
trying to live his life without a heart.

Girls Taking Showers at a Summer Camp

They're not like ordinary voices,
where the glum information of reality
slithers from indifferent lips.
Their voices cannot help but rise
into song and remain there, as high
as birds fly, and then descend once more
after the laughter. The soap foams,
backs glisten, the shapely legs
under the partition move
the way deer move in the night,
barely touching the earth.

A hush of holiness pervades the pines,
as if some Roman goddess
were bathing behind the leaves,
guarded by other girls equally lovely.
If I were honest, I would say
my eyes were as heavy as bullets
in my head, each time turning away
from higher things, like my soul's journey,
and gazing once more on the forbidden
glitter of a day in paradise.

After Sunday Service

After church, everyone is saved again.
It's early, and the sun is pouring
through the windows like waterfalls of gold.
You can't make a mistake right now;
you're blessed, your hand still smells
of the cologne from the preacher's hand.
You have that grace about you, a kind
of daisy-glow, incandescent for those
who were with you that morning.

You say hello to strangers; you give
your daughter a dollar to spend
"however she wishes." It's okay, you say,
"we can afford this once in a while."
Oh church, the stones of rectitude
hold my faith together, and bolt down
a roof in which grace is collected.
The gentle folk that worship beside you
make the world lighter, an airy palace
of hopes and opportunities.

And home is filled with the sweetness
of the dead, who have passed through
these rooms and left behind their trust.
How they love you still, how they
reach out a ghost hand and pat your back,
and tell you the road to the cemetery
may be long, but in time, you will be there
to celebrate the opening of the glorious gates.

But Monday looms over you like a tower
of Babel. Windows are filled with foreign faces

glaring at you, watching the street with fear.
There's trouble in the world; you hear rumors
of restless nations spawning terrorists
who might one day aim a rifle at your heart.
You have neighbors you don't like.
They laugh and drink into the night.
Who knows what malice
thrives in their twisted hearts?

The Ugly Land

I'm catching my second breath
above the Brazos. Rocks are fairly rare
this way along, where the earth is full
of clay and shells. Caddoans found
no shelter here; even Karankawas
were leery of the beasts that roamed,
the insects that ate the flesh off a man's bones.
Better to harvest the seashore of its crabs
and crayfish, the wild berries
that fed Cabeza de Vaca later on.
No, this is hostile country, and I'm tired
of its monotony, the short
grass as harsh as a stray dog's hair.

But it's land with a stubborn will,
that flung off all its parasites in time.
You have to give it credit for surviving
the greed of waves of settlers.
No one found the place
worth farming. It's as primitive as
the lava beds of Big Bend further west,
and buried in its flesh are secrets
no one wants to know. The origins
are written here, in the ghostly script
of the wind, and the grass that trembles
like the surf of a vanished shore.
You come here to settle your hash,
to pay the price of hard-heartedness,
and a stingy soul.

The more flawed you are, the better
to face this altar of atonement,

to lie back onto the prickly grass
and feel the pain of martyrs and saints.
Shame on you, says the dull brown
land as it wags a mesquite switch
in your face. The buzzards are amused.
The bees are curious but move on.
Ants have built their mansion
in your abandoned conscience
and will not scare, even when you shout.

What the Poor Are Doing in Texas

Dreams are like little blistered doors
leading out of a bedroom. No one knows
about them. You have to be asleep to open one.
Once inside, you grope your way down a long
wooden corridor. The walls are made of
splintery shiplap, and a single light bulb
hangs over you like an eye, dusty and
moth clotted. A chain pulls the circuit open
and dim light bleeds into the air.
A board creaks and the snoring
behind the wall stops, and then resumes.

The police know you are in there.
They have seen the light go on, which
gilds the louvers of an attic ventilator.
They touch their holsters as they wait below.
Someone brings sandwiches and the talk
is all about the dreamers trying to escape.
Maybe this time one of them will come
rattling down a drain pipe, a mouth
full of diamond necklaces, pockets full of golden rings.

You never know how hard it is to get
to the end of this narrow passage.
You're not the first to try.
They say this is an old track in the sand
once walked by nomads with their camels.
I've heard it said that hominids came
down from the trees and walked for
the first time, and found the corridor endless.
In dreams begin the journey, the longest one
in life. If you are poor, you take it anyway.
You have no choice. No choice. No choice.

At Home

My aging body fascinates me.
The skin that holds my breath
and memories is crocheted with wrinkles,
the road map of all my weary years.

I am sitting in a chair reading
Chinese history, and the woodcuts
illuminate the life of a palace –
lanterns swaying in the wind,
the sloping roof dripping
with icy rain, men seated
on pillows in the broad hall.

I have been there in my dreams,
and I long to return some day.
But right now, my hand is under
the lamp and I see rice padis
forming over my thumb.

Have you ever tried to terrace a mountainside?
If not, you are missing something.
The padis glow like shards of mirror
in the twilight, and their irregular
shapes are like the plates on a turtle's back.

And the turtle moves slowly, the way
I do when I get up at night and pad
to the bathroom to lean against
the wall and empty my aching bladder.

I am an old farmer with a hoe propped
by the door, as a Chinese sun

just now begins to rise out
of the rose-petaled morning.
It hangs there over Fort Worth,
and the stark glass towers
are melting into gardens, and the
mountains are covered with the emperor's jewels.

III

I Used to Be So Sure about You

Forty years of marriage would have ruined
most friendships. Consider a wallet,
a pair of shoes, a tie, they don't last long.
Time gnaws with little teeth
at everything. I have a marble from childhood
that rolls around in my desk drawer
when I'm looking for the scissors.

It's nicked, fogged with old age.
It can't be accurate anymore, no matter
how I might hold my thumb against it.
A shooter lasts a year or two and ends
up in a cigar box with your brass whistle.

Remember that when you're a child;
your shoes will be on the far side
of the universe by the time you enter college.
Your love life will be fading in a frame,
eaten by invisible mouths, and left there
to mock your most cherished memories.

But marriage has not removed us from the play.
We're still there reciting our lines, coming
in and out of the script
with business to conduct,
children to raise. I have kissed you like this
in act three a million times, and each time
your mouth is eager and partly open,
your eyes tearing up with affection.

The audience is nervous, waiting for action.
We must keep the plot moving as best we can.

But look, the lamps making sunlight
in the living room window are not as bright.
The spot in which I speak my lines
is yellowing a little; maybe it's the gel
they haven't replaced in the last few years.

Your dress has a tear, and I noticed it
the other night. I meant to tell the seamstress.
Our son is off to war; he intends to marry
the girl next door, even though the house
is invisible and the girl never walked this earth.
Pity us here, on stage, creaking around
with lines to say, and no matter how often
we say them, they're always different.

When the curtain falls and the clapping dies,
we stand there like two strangers, wondering
what to do now that the stage is dark.
I know! We'll eat dinner out tonight
and toast our marriage. I don't know you
like I did before; you keep revealing
things I didn't think a woman cared about.
Strange thoughts, secrets the heart
prefers to keep to itself. But there it is,
the body beside me in bed a dark country
full of villages that never sleep, but
murmur and teach cockatiels how to count,
and make supper ground from taro roots.

Old Friends and Poets

My friends keep disappearing
like soldiers on a long march,
drifting off into the trees
to hide from the sergeant,
never returning.

Take my old friend Paul Foreman,
who used to hunt for gold
in California, in the river beds
below collapsed *calderas*.
He had a loupe in his pocket
for examining the flecks of platinum.

He knew more about geology
than most professors; they admitted it.
He wandered the ground like
an old mystic, eyes poring
over the open book of a dry gulley.
He loved volcanoes. He loved Homer, too.

Ricardo Sanchez comes to mind.
A bear of a man with enough anger
to fuel a rocket ship to get him
to the moon and back.
He had his grudges, but his mercies
were thick in his chest.
He loved his life, and words
poured out of him like torrents
in the rainy season.
He ate his eggs in a swamp
of salsa and lime, and *jalapeños*.
He wasn't bitter he said, just vigilant.

And Jim Cody, the red-haired incendiary
of Austin, whom I first met
climbing over the backs of folding chairs
trying to get to Dave Oliphant,
to finish a quarrel in Scots-Irish style.
They were not matched for fighting.
Dave is lean, correct, immaculate
in ironed slacks and brand-new loafers.
Cody was a mess, an orangutan
swinging through the trees
on the slopes of Parnassus, chanting
Irish lyrics and gazing fondly
on the rivers he went camping on.
My old friend was gentle under
all the bluster, and faithful to the end.

Bill Burford has drifted off the hill
where he pored over books of Greek statues
and the lost world of Byzantium.
He had kept the temple lamps lit
for many years in exile,
his lonely life in the last half of the century.
The pale cottages that ranged below him
sheltered the ordinary souls
of Ft. Worth, while he honed
his eyes and ears on the sublime passion
of Sappho and Bion. I miss him, too.

A Dinner Party in the Hills

The dinner party was all about politics,
the hated Republican majority,
the shameful nature of red states
and the Deep South. A woman next
to me put down her fork and stood up.
"As a black woman," she began,
but no one was listening.
She tried to go on but the hostess
asked the maid if there was more coffee.
Someone lit a cigar and left
to stand on the porch. I had ham
left on my plate and a man took
it with his fingers and ate it, smiling at me.

A large house perched on the crest of
a gorge, with sleek black cars
parked in the horseshoe-drive.
Someone was playing the piano
in the sun room, Broadway songs,
a ballad of the old west, an Indian love song.
We listened and the black woman
who was going to make her point
sat down again, spreading her napkin
on her lap. It was late in the afternoon,
everyone present a success in some way,
a few writers, some professors, a doctor,
the forlorn Democrat from Rockhart
who had lost the election. He was eager
to go home and have a drink, and think
about his future. The rest of us listened
to the piano and thought about our past.

The pulse of Texas beat deep below the earth,
in a cave where a tired river struggled
to flow east to the Gulf. It was old,
and the farmers upstream had robbed
its force to water sorghum fields.
We have made mistakes, terrible errors
in our stewardship, I wanted to say,
but like the black woman beside me,
it wasn't the time. It wasn't the place.

Moses on the Outskirts of Austin

I know a man who argues with the birds
when he's out wandering the hills.
They fly over him and look down
with mean eyes, and caw his name
in their guttural dialect. He shouts
back his curses at them, hand raised
in fury. He owns the land, he tells them.
It's been his for generations, deeds
and old papers attest to the fact.

He can't put the vast declines into his pocket.
He has no means for gathering up
the trees and carting them home
to his backyard. The clouds, all crazy
in the air in their drunk shapes,
don't come at his call. The wind
is its own master much of the time.
When it rains, the low places fill first
and the hard earth lets the rest
of the water run off into ditches,
never to return. But in human form,
clutching his rights in his right hand,
he is lord and master of all he sees.

* * *

The cry of a child's voice under the sky
echoes with all its human frailty.
Such slivers of sound thread mortality
on a spool and dangle a soul
over the abyss. Not even a shadow
is cast by its flimsy coat of flesh,

its bones. Its petition to exist goes
unheard into the vaulted heavens.

But there he stands, a desperate
inquisitor into the will of nature,
demanding an answer to his question:
Who really owns the world?
But on he walks, disconsolate,
head down watching his feet
measure the distance he covers
in infinity, his wrist watch
peeling off the seconds from eternity.

Let's Build Some Temples

The woods are like holocaust survivors
after the loggers came through.
Small, meager saplings with their
bark sheared off by tractor treads;
a bent, half-broken juniper, that desert
warrior, gasping for air, robbed
of its powerful soul by fire a year ago.

The road that pulled out the logs
is still raw, torn up like some
lunatic had been plowing
the earth with a Russian tank.
Birds are rare, and the few that live
here are sulking and scrawny.

But the wood is singing under
the saw as I speak. The slabs
fall off onto the conveyor belt
and sail into the planer,
the finish blade, and head for the kiln
to be pressed with creosote.
No longer tree at all, but the skin
of some human house for a generation.

Bacchus is drunk somewhere far away,
lying on the moss with his lovers
and musicians, waving
a hand at all the wilderness
he is the guardian of, the great muse
of poetry and inspiration.
Were there more gods to pray to,
we might survive another year.

Thirteen Ways of Looking at a Grackle

1.

A grackle sits on a bench at a funeral parlor preening its blue-black feathers.

2.

The telephone wires are swollen with roosting birds. The sky is jet black behind them, and below their toothpick feet, the sun lies on its deathbed above the suburbs.

3.

The Walmart parking lot is an aviary of black birds; they do not believe in freedom, only the windfalls of self-indulgence.

4.

When a grackle flies, a widow ends her grief and takes a lover.

5.

Blackbird soup is a delicacy in hell.

6.

My neighbor shot a grackle with a .22 rifle one morning, after listening to its rusty hinge all night.

7.

When grackles court, other birds listen as if their own deaths were being mourned by blind men with broken flutes.

8.

A grackle hops on wooden crutches, and tucks his razor and soap under his left wing. He is a born drifter and longs for the moan of the freight train.

9.

A blackbird coughed up phlegm as black as chimney soot, wiped it on his chest and flew slowly skyward to roost on a church steeple.

10.

I have seen a grackle sleeping in a hole in a wall where a brick had fallen. They have been known to make a house out of a tire, an abandoned mailbox, the wood pile of the minister, the gap in a cistern lid, an old man's hat left on a park bench, the back porch of a woman in a wheel chair.

11.

Grackles were birds of paradise in Atlantis. The emperor kept two on his lap when he ate dinner, and they sang folk songs to him long into the evening.

12.

The laughter of children in a street is the only human sound that makes a grackle listen.

13.

Love is a tiered cake, a reception on a hotel roof full of well-wishers, and a cloudy sky where grackles hang their feet and look down.

The Geography of the Brain

Gary Snyder called it the "back country,"
the place where dreams arise
and come to us clothed in our memories.
We toss and turn, waking
the voices of childhood and the wilderness
they now live in. Go far enough
into the woods, and fairy tales begin.

Freud poked with a learned pencil
into the quick of our minds,
and found life so primitive
it lacked a name. Call it the "it," he wrote,
that latitude of dinosaurs and pterodactyls
in a Jurassic reserve.

My daughter saw a bear on the way
to Silver Lake last summer, and ran
down the hill for her life. A brown bear,
shaggy, thick-clawed, a mouth
fenced with sharp incisors around a hungry tongue.
He didn't chase her; his home was
in her dreams, he said.

You'll have to lie in bed a long while
to get such creatures to reveal themselves.

Meanwhile, the first street carved
into the woods defined where language
starts, where numbers begin to count,
where alienation builds its walls
to keep our children safe.

At Night I Give up My Soul

Something steals over me at night
like a cloak full of star holes,
and a rip that gapes open
big as the moon.
I grieve at the weight of the cloth
holding me down from dreaming.
I feel the scrape of dead
planets plunging through my mind,
and the longing heaven fills me with.

In the morning, I put on fresh sunlight
like a white shirt, and shave in the mirror
where gold concentrates from the sky.
I am alive again, a man out of his grave
for a walk through the countryside.
It's easy to mistake the ground for
some offering of kindness from the dead.

I suffer the stares of strangers
as I pass, but I turn them into moths
and butterflies. Nothing slows my feet
because the bed I must lie upon
is close behind. I need the embrace
of someone's arms to comfort me.
When I am heading up the stairs
I hear the weaver's loom sighing
with thread, as a shuttle
full of ghosts ferries back and forth
across the ancient sky.

The Man Who Talked too Much

Once, when I walked the city
like anyone else, I was eager
to speak my mind, even to strangers.
I had opinions like someone else
has coins in his pocket.
I felt liberated each time I spoke.

Others stopped to listen, and moved
on smiling sympathetically.
They all agreed with me.
I had the last word on the ways
of this fallen world. I knew the future
like some old women know the past.
I could count on my imagination
to guide me. I had a voice inside
that always spoke the truth.

But when the paradox of my own
existence occurred to me, a weak
flame caught in the cold north wind
each winter, and saw the glow
sputter and go out, it left me
in a corner of the room
afraid to speak, afraid to admit
I want to live, at any cost.

Chores

There's an art to sweeping.
It's in the wrists, the way you plant
your feet, inches apart for balance,
letting the hips swivel a little
as you gather the dust
to the lip of a dust pan
and then urge all your errors
and regrets to join the dirt
and vanish in a can.

Every family has a history
of misunderstandings,
rough words at dinner,
resentments that last for years.
They all fall to the floor
and disintegrate, darken
the carpet, line the threshold
with a kind of haze, which
the broom will harvest one day.

The Romans called it the lustrum,
the smoke time, when evil
spirits were driven out
by the harsh fog of a torch.
Some tribes burned their huts
to winnow out the germs.
Ganesh, the rogue elephant
of India, crushed every living trace
of human malice from the earth.

It all comes back like bad pennies,
of course. The house whiles away

a summer in glorious sunshine,
the fragrance of the flowers
in the window sill, the curtains
blowing in to let the world
empty out its box of spells
upon the sofa, the rug, and then
we wait for spring to sweep them out.

Walking Behind Terlingua

There are ghosts in the rock;
their grimaces appear after a rain.
You may be strolling along, singing
a wordless tune to yourself,
when you look up and behold
the dead gazing down at you,
like gargoyles on a cathedral wall.

It startles the heart,
and wakens nerves long idle
in the back of your memory.
What does it mean, you ask yourself,
as if waking from a life-long slumber.
"I don't know," you mutter.

Your feet can hardly lift off the ground;
the car seems so far away in its patch
of sunlight. All the pleasures
of the day abandon you like birds
rising from a marsh.
You are alone, as alone as you ever were before.
Cliffs rise steeply around you,
as if you stared from the bottom of a grave.

Love and Death

A man has two dogs he calls
love and death. They are inseparable.
One will run into the dark woods
and the other waits up for him,
sometimes all night long. In the morning,
out of nowhere, death comes home
and sits on the doorstep, hungry,
while love licks her paws.

In a field with a broken fence
at the far end, love and death
chase each other. The old man
admires the reckless leaps
love makes to keep up, and the wily
skill of death to hide from her.

When he calls, only love comes
trotting back, her tail low, her eyes
smarting from the whips of grass.
Death is staying out
where the wind blows from the north,
where winter keeps a modest house
and will not stir until the end of fall.

To Grow Old in Texas

When you are here long enough
your face turns to granite. You smile
but nothing happens. Strangers
are uncomfortable around you,
unless they have lived here
as long as you have. Then jaws
move, and eyes blink suddenly,
and hands go out to be shaken.

But the granite tightens like
a headache around you.
You have paid the price.
The ground has fallen in love
with you, and reaches up
with mineral arms and sedentary
affections to hold you.
It's not meant to alarm you,
but to tell you, at last, you belong.

Now your footsteps don't echo
or leave a print behind. You stand
in the early morning with the wind
passing through you.
A garden leans forward to touch
you as you walk, and you go on
like a beautiful old woman,
a celebrity among the arroyos.
The sky is your hat, and the rain
enfolds you in a silver coat.
You belong, you belong!

When the birds cry overhead,
they mean to say hello
in their prehistoric language.
You can't answer, of course,
but your landscape is as gray
and mottled as the desert,
and they merely want to know
where you are going.

Sixty years of solemn afternoons,
sixty summers of curtains lifting slowly,
sixty winters of glazed eaves
and myopic windows,
sixty springs of anguish and desertion.
These anneal the flesh and make
a leather pouch for the soul to rattle in.

Your bones grind in their sockets,
and your eyes click like beetles
when you blink. Your hands trace
the veins of quartz in the sandstone,
where blood ran hot a million years ago.
Forgive what fate has given to you.
It points its finger blindly at the child
and slows its feet, binds its hope
to a catalog of sunsets and long nights.

The Hunt

A coyote lies in the half-dead prairie
waiting for a hare to go out looking
for his supper. His fur matches the thirsty
dirt, the weeds. He closes his eyes
and hears the ground through his skinny paws.
He's about to fall asleep when the hare
makes his first, tentative move.
The soft, sleek body tenses up,
the muscular hind legs flex and recoil
in a beautiful jump, three feet
off the ground, a sudden brown blur
graceful as a butterfly, already
reloading his feet for a second leap.

Such beauty is rare, happens like rain fall
or a rainbow stretching over the skin-iced river.
It's the equivalent of falling in love,
meeting some stranger's eyes
for the first time and feeling
a rush of heart into a tongue-tied mouth.

The hare is wide-eyed, savvy,
he knows where the coyote hides.
He sees him at the back of his imagination
and comes to earth only to bound again,
even higher. The sky is like a plate
of steel, curved and on fire
at its rim, as the sun cuts
a molten path where night comes through.

The coyote is as pious as a saint,
meaning no harm to any living thing.

He barely flicks a single muscle of his back
as the hare flies over him, an angel
in fur and airy bones, a virtuous creature
on his way to a rendezvous with larks.
Until the coyote twists his muscles
into a knot and shoots himself high
up to meet the hare head on, with
a crunch of his sparkling fangs
and a satisfying burst of bone and blood.

A West Texas Marriage

A woman who lived out of town
married an eagle after her husband died.
She owned the ranch, and raised
some cows for beef. The river was dry
and she pumped a well to keep the beasts alive.
It never rained on her roof; the garden
died the death of a tortured prisoner.
The road was ruts and seldom raised
its dust, unless the mailman made his run.

The eagle was cold, and stared at her
in bed, and barely touched her shoulder
when they joined bodies to make love.
He was unsentimental as a philosopher,
a creature whose thinking flew him
higher than the moon at times,
and made him a guest of the tops of mountains.
She cooked the supper, tended to the wash,
while he came home with a rattlesnake
in his talons, or the carcass of a lamb.

They seldom spoke; she loved him in her way,
and he loved back, without affection.
He was not of her kind, he said,
and she replied he was. She had her visions, too,
she said, and pulled him to her.
The world went on without them,
and they lived in wordless peace.

He left for days at a time, and flew
to places she did not know existed.
When he returned, he took his bath

in the yard, and lay back exhausted from his journey. Love in the desert is never easy; it lives on torment and disappointment, a daily dose of venom from a snake, and a yucca blossom when you least expect it.

Is It Ten o' Clock Yet?

I hear mothers calling for their children.
Their lonely voices sing into the night.
The trees hold ignorance in their fists,
and the owls are eager to catch the unwary
mole wandering home alone.
Here, logic loosens its ancient grip
and lets slip a dream or two,
and the monsters roam the edges
of thought, licking at the fragile
boundary between common sense
and madness. One by one the short-sleeve
shirts appear, the summer shoes,
the slow-burning eyes of children
who have not lost their innocence.

The night gives them up reluctantly;
they have much to learn from fear,
and the mistakes that lie buried
in the cemetery, and rise at midnight
to haunt the living world.
The fruit of ignorance is swollen
and ripe, but no one will eat it now.
The grass talks to the worms,
and the wind falls in love with
a street lamp orbited by moths.
Every danger stands on hind legs
looking on, as the mothers
grow impatient and sharpen their voices.
Nothing is sacred in this dying
light, with the earth drowning
at their feet, and the islands
coming to the surface like first sleep.

The Cascades of Autumn

Fall has begun to dismantle itself.
The towers are leaning, the grass
fades like old love letters.
I lost the path I took to school;
it lies under the leaves like so much
homework, so many notes
I threw away. I smell the first
fire on the mountain, a smell
that makes the heart stand still
long enough to think of death.

Such paltry things as roses
show no rectitude; they give in
the moment the stars tilt north,
and drop their constellations.
The daisies are all gone; they
flew away with their boyfriends
after the prom. Someone bangs
on a drum in the cellar, trying
to call the saints from their tombs.
I light a candle and stare at it
until my eyes go blind; only
then can you begin to imagine
the world as a place of spirits.

Fall is a lonely time, with space
at the end of the bench for strangers.
The streets are empty; I seldom
hear a car after six p.m.
I wish there were more seasons
than the four that age us.
There ought to be some epilogue

to summer, some rhyming speech
about the goals of love, the purpose
of a beating heart, a panting
pair of lips eager to be kissed again.
But we close the book, and someone
lights a fire that will burn
all night, and then we wake up cold.

A Poem for my Father

Out on a prairie, a boy
leans over his father's knee
to be whipped until his legs
are red with welts.
The sky is as hard as enamel
on a Turkish vase, and so
is the boy's heart, now that
his father lets him go.

The ground is a magical dimension
as it climbs the hill;
you can catch the moon up there.
You can't bring it home
or your father will take off
his belt and teach you a lesson
about stealing. So, best leave
the magic where it hangs
over the maize fields,
the wisps of clouds as they
head west like so many mustangs
on the run. You close your
heart the way an old woman
locks her pantry from prying
fingers, eager to taste her apple jam.

In the old days of gaiters
and spats, and gray fedoras
on men's heads, and corsets
that made your grandmother's breath
creak like a sailing ship,
you could walk to the fence line
and back and no one would

know you were even gone.
There were Indians roaming the land
with their herds of sheep,
and old Mexican traders who
walked in the paths of the *comancheros*.

You ate your corn cake and slurped
up the pool of blackberry water
with your spoon, and looked
out to see the moon rising
like a Spanish galleon setting sail for heaven.

In the Depths behind El Paso

Here's the highway. As flat as Euclid's
geometry, stricter than Descartes' method.
It lacks all doubt about its destination,
due west into a burning desert banked
with low-lying fire-scorched clouds.

On the side, in a trench of dark shadow,
is a gasoline station, the sign long
gone on the south winds of spring.
A rusty dog lies still on the pavement.
A boy grew up here and took the bus
to a city, never to return. The old man
survived the death of his wife, a daughter.

The one lone car coming into view
is splitting the brilliance of the day
in slivers, scattering diamonds
behind it on its way to oblivion.
A cloud would be more comfort
in this silence. Or a wind. Something
to rattle the tin sheets of the roof
and make a bit of music.

What lived upon the land conceals
its memory in a parched stain
of fossils. They flake away in the arms
of time, and leave the past erased.

A truck carrying supplies stops to unload,
and for an hour life returns. Words
are spoken, the bill paid, a hand shaken.
Then the great canopy of sky

stretches on its invisible tendons
and holds the earth in place.
What the soul yearns for
has no name, but it trembles in the air.
Like the ghosts who roam here after dark,
there is always motion under the stars,
a restless urge of every missing thing.

The Loneliest Tuesday of the Year

My mother is a blue flame
on the window sill. There's no talking
to her now; she's gone, as far away
as there are stranded galaxies
on the edge of the night sky.
But she's there, a lighted tongue
of blue air, like the flame over which
she cooked our dinner, reheated
the coffee in a red pot, boiled water.
A blue flame, but no way to reach her.

The children are standing in the cemetery
below the house, singing, gathering flowers.
They have been let out of school early
and told to go home. They have no key
to their doors, no reason to sit
in the desolate afternoon light
to wait for a mother to return.
So they gather here, among the cold stones
and pick flowers, stuff them into cracked
vases, try to right the leaning crosses.

Our measure of light would fill a water glass.
We get our lips wet on the sun,
our eyes bathe in the glitter before us,
but we are given so little, and beg for more.

www.ingramcontent.com/pod-product-compliance
Lightning Source LLC
Chambersburg PA
CBHW020946090426
42736CB00010B/1283